EXPOSING JACK THE STRIPPER

A BIOGRAPHY OF THE WORST SERIAL
KILLER YOU'VE PROBABLY NEVER
HEARD OF

FERGUS MASON

Absolute Crime Press
ANAHEIM, CALIFORNIA

Contents

ABOUT ABSOLUTE CRIME

Absolute Crime publishes only the best true crime literature. Our focus is on the crimes that you've probably never heard of, but you are fascinated to read more about. With each engaging and gripping story, we try to let readers relive moments in history that some people have tried to forget.

Remember, our books are not meant for the faint at heart. We don't hold back--if a crime is bloody, we let the words splatter across the page so you can experience the crime in the most horrifying way!

If you enjoy this book, please visit our homepage (www.AbsoluteCrime.com) to see other books we offer; if you have any feedback, we'd love to hear from you!

INTRODUCTION

"Jack the Stripper? You're having a laugh, right?"

I could understand the librarian's confusion. If I'd asked for information about Jack the Ripper I'd have been on solid ground; everyone has heard of the mysterious killer who stalked London's Whitechapel district in 1888, committing a series of five increasingly atrocious mutilation murders that stopped as suddenly and mysteriously as it had begun. The Ripper was never caught. Despite hundreds of books and academic papers on the subject his identity still isn't known a century and a quarter after his final crime. That hasn't stopped people from speculating, of course; there are now more than a hundred theories about who was behind the crimes and why. "Ripperology" is still big business, with a ready market for any new and interesting look at the notorious crimes. Conspiracy theorists have had a field day, especially with the mysterious graffiti that announced, "The Juwes are the ones who will not be blamed for nothing." Was it the work of an illiterate anti-Semite – or a coded warning from a Freemason?[1]

I wasn't researching Jack the Ripper though. This time I was looking for information about a less well-known but equally ruthless killer, who between 1964 and 1965 left the nude bodies of six prostitutes scattered round Hammersmith. Two previous murders were probably his work too, and there's a real possibility that he had started killing more than 40 years earlier. This maniac preferred to strangle rather than slash,

---

[1] In Masonic imagery the Master Mason, Hiram Abiff, was murdered by three young apprentices named – somewhat improbably - Jubela, Jubelo and Jubelum. Collectively they are known as the Juwes. The Ripper's spelling has caused much speculation about Masonic connections.

but he killed with the same single-minded determination as the notorious Ripper. Like his almost-namesake there is speculation about his identity and a few suspects, but nobody was ever arrested and there's no hard evidence either way.

Jack the Stripper never achieved the fame of the 19th century killer, but he hasn't been completely forgotten. Over the decades since his mysterious killing spree ended several researchers have looked into the case, and some of them have made intriguing suggestions about his identity. Unless some new piece of evidence comes to light – and that doesn't seem likely – we'll never know for sure who he was. All we can be certain of is what he did.

Of course there's nothing all that remarkable about a serial killer who stalks prostitutes. It's a sad fact that ladies of negotiable affection make easy targets because their profession demands that they go off alone with men they don't know, and the law doesn't always pay their deaths the attention it should. Six – or even eight – isn't even that high a death toll for a serial killer. Instead of remarking that Jack the Stripper hasn't been completely forgotten you could wonder why he's remembered at all. In fact there are several reasons why the case continues to fascinate people. London is one of the world's oldest and greatest cities; murder is something usually associated with its slums, and when nude bodies start turning up in respectable neighborhoods or floating down the Thames people tend to take notice. The brutal nature of the deaths helps, and of course there's always an element of mystery about serial killers who evaded capture. The Stripper case also has hints of a bigger picture, of connections between the sordid business conducted by street prostitutes and the glamorous upper reaches of London society. It even touches on a scandal that extended into the British government.

For all its brutality and squalor the story of Jack the Stripper is a fascinating one. Researching it brought a new understanding of 1960s London and the dark currents that flowed beneath its surface. Reading about it may have the same effect, so let's dive in to those currents and see where they lead. And don't be surprised when you turn the page - the story begins forty years earlier and hundreds of miles away, in rural Wales.

[1]

THE KILLINGS BEGIN

Abertillery, Wales: Sunday, February 6, 1921

Fred Burnell was frantic with worry. Early the day before his 8-year-old daughter Freda had left home to run an errand to the local store, and hadn't come home. A visit to Mortimer's Grain Store had confirmed that she'd been there – she'd been the first customer in fact, turning up at five after nine, then leaving at quarter past. Where had she gone then? The young shop assistant told Fred he didn't know. The store was located on Somerset Street, a residential road lined with small, neat row houses built from brick and gray local stone. Abertillery had grown quickly over the last 30 years as workers flooded in to the new coalmines – from a large village of 10,000 in 1891 it was now a tightly packed town of nearly 40,000. Despite the rapid expansion it was still a close community, though. The hard, dangerous life of the men working down in the pits brought families together, and prompted people to look out for their neighbors; nobody knew when they'd need support because a husband was injured or trapped below ground, so it was natural for people to look out for each other. If any of the residents down Somerset Street had seen Freda they'd have got word to Burnell, and most likely walked her straight home.

Burnell spent six hours searching the streets for his daughter, but as the afternoon wore on and the sun dropped lower in the sky he admitted defeat and went to the police to report her missing. It wasn't long before the local force were out on the streets, knocking on doors and asking questions. A wave of concern swept through Abertillery and search parties were quickly organized. It was getting late, though, and the weather was cold. The search began well after three o'clock, and by quarter past five the sun had set. The searchers stayed out until midnight before giving up in the face of the darkness and weather. It was a long night for Fred Burnell; he had no idea where his daughter was, and the thought of a small child perhaps wandering lost in the bitter weather must have been torture for him. The searchers were worried too; at first light they were back out on the hills around the town.

It wasn't the police or the search parties who found Freda, though. Just before sunrise a collier, making the morning coal delivery, saw a bundle of rags on the lane behind Duke Street. That wasn't too unusual, but something made him take a closer look. That was a decision he almost instantly regretted.

The bundle of rags was the body of Freda Burnell, and she'd clearly been the victim of a savage attack. The police quickly concluded that she'd been raped and murdered, and a doctor concluded that she'd died not long after her disappearance.2 The Abertillery police were used to keeping order in the sometimes tough streets of a mining town, but an atrocity like this alarmed them; they called for help from Scotland Yard, and a team of London detectives arrived to join the investigation.

The key to finding Freda's killer was to trace her movements after she'd left Mortimer's Grain Store, and every inquiry was drawing a blank; nobody remembered seeing her after she'd left the store. The search began to narrow its focus, and when a witness claimed to have heard screams coming from a shed behind the store alarm bells started to ring. The police searched the shed and found Freda's handkerchief, along with an ax. There was only one key to the shed and it was held by the young assistant who'd spoken to Fred Burnell the day Freda died, 15-year-old Harold Jones. On February 10, Jones was arrested and

---

2 Murderpedia, Harold Jones
    http://www.murderpedia.org/male.J/j/jones-harold.htm

charged with murder. His trial began in Monmouth Assizes on June 17, and lasted for four days. The Scotland Yard detectives firmly believed Jones was the killer, but the evidence against him was purely circumstantial and his denials couldn't be disproven. There was no choice - he was found not guilty. When he returned to Abertillery many locals joined him in celebrating; they refused to believe that one of their own could have been responsible. George Little told him, "Well done son, we knew you didn't do it."

Just 17 days after Jones's acquittal, on July 8, Little's daughter Florrie disappeared. For two days terrified parents sheltered their children as search parties walked the hills around town, but no trace of the 11-year-old was found. On July 10 police began a door-to-door search through the town.3 When they knocked on Philip Jones's door he invited them in and

---

3 Serial Killer Crime Index, JONES Harold
    http://www.crimezzz.net/serialkillers/J/ JONES_harold.php

stood by as they searched; of course it was his duty to help find the missing girl. His son Harold didn't share his feelings though, and quietly slipped out of the house. When one of the constables pushed open the trapdoor leading from the boy's bedroom and looked into the attic, then gave a horrified yell, Philip Jones realized the appalling truth and dashed into the streets in search of his son. He managed to catch him, and personally turned him in to the constabulary. Once again Harold Jones was put on trial at Monmouth Assizes, and this time he confessed.

He'd killed Freda Burnell, he said, because he had a "desire to kill." After his release he'd lured Florrie Little to his home while his parents were out. He'd then assaulted her, cut her throat, bled her out over the kitchen sink and concealed her body in the attic.4 His parents had come home before he'd been able to dispose of it properly and with the town being searched he hadn't had a chance since. It was clear that what Jones was talking about was a pair of premeditated murders, and there was no chance of a not guilty verdict this time. The only option open was the sentence. At the time of the verdict Jones was two months short of his 16th birthday. If he'd been tried after that date there's little doubt he would have been hanged. As it was he was sentenced to be detailed "At His Majesty's Pleasure." In effect that means an indefinite jail term. In the end he served 20 years in Usk Jail – just ten miles from Abertillery – then in London's Wandsworth Prison. In 1941 he applied for parole and, despite objections from the prison's psychiatrist

4 Wales Online, Nov 25, 2007, Author names new killer in Drinkwater case

http://www.walesonline.co.uk/news/wales-news/author-names-new-killer-drinkwater-2220319

and governor, he got it. Aged 35 he was freed back into society, changed his name and vanished.

Mortlake, London: November 8, 1963

Walk down Thames Bank in London's Mortlake district – a pleasant, leafy street running along the side of the river – and you'll come to The Ship, a traditional old English pub with big bay windows and baskets of flowers decorating the exterior. Most evenings the varnished bar is full of locals, but if you're lucky enough to get good weather for your visit there's an alternative. Beside the attractive building with its blue and white paintwork is a beer garden, where you can enjoy a drink outside. It's a pleasant place to sit on a sunny day; it's been renovated recently and nicely landscaped, and you can relax there despite being in the middle of one of the world's busiest cities. If you know the history of that patch of ground, though, some dark thoughts can creep in. That's even truer if you're there to learn about Jack the Stripper.

In the early 1960s Mortlake housed working class families and the workshops and warehouses that employed them, along with a transient population attracted by relatively low rents. Gentrification hadn't yet begun and nobody was going to call it an attractive area, but it was respectable enough. Redevelopment hadn't quite sorted out the damage done by the war, though. German bombers lost over London often used the Thames as an aiming mark for their bombs, and Mortlake had suffered its share of destruction. Vacant lots, known as bombsites, were a feature of many British cities for decades after the war. When the rubble was cleared residents often put them to use as parking lots, play areas or informal dumps. As land values in London rose they began to get cleaned up and redeveloped, and on this Friday morning a crew of city workmen had come to clear away a trash dump beside The Ship.

It was dirty work; as well as domestic garbage the patch was heaped with rotting produce discarded by local traders. The cleanup crew was used to it though, and protected by coveralls and rubber boots they got on with it cheerfully enough. Load by load the festering mess was shoveled into wheelbarrows, run up a plank and tipped into the back of the Corporation truck. When the smell got too bad they retreated to a fire built from scrap timber, drank strong tea brewed in a blackened kettle, smoked a cigarette and then got back to the task. And then they found something horrible.

A swung shovel, instead of scooping up a few pounds of loose garbage, splatted into something soft but heavy. At the same time a revolting stench erupted from the pit. Perhaps wondering if he'd unearthed a dead dog a workman cleared the rubbish away – and exposed the partly decomposed body of a woman. They could tell it was a woman; it was naked apart from a single nylon stocking.

In any big city decomposed bodies turn up from time to time. Many are old or ill people who die at home alone. Others are the homeless who, driven beyond endurance by sickness or weather, crawl into shelter and never come out again. A stripped corpse buried in a midden was different, though. Most likely it meant murder; it definitely meant crime of some description, if nothing else because burying bodies in a dump is always illegal. The Metropolitan Police knew that the scene was too disturbed for much in the way of clues to be found, so they looked to learn what they could from the body.

It didn't take long before they established the dead woman's identity. She was 22-year-old Gwynneth Rees, a former teenage runaway from south Wales who'd ended up selling herself in London. She'd last been seen alive getting into a van on September 29, which tied in with the state of her body. Other working girls told the police that when she disappeared she'd been pregnant and had been looking for an illegal abortionist.[5] At first that seemed a possible explanation for her death; perhaps she'd died during an illegal termination and the

---

[5] Until 1967 anyone carrying out, or having, an abortion in the UK could be sentenced to life in prison. Since then it has been legal on health grounds if two doctors agree.

abortionist had panicked and disposed of her body. The autopsy on her corpse suggested something different, though. Several teeth were missing and the mark of a strangling ligature was found around her neck. That meant it was definitely murder. More streetwalkers were questioned: Had Rees upset anyone before she vanished? It turned out she had. Her "ponce" (pimp) had been Cornelius "Connie" Whitehead, a minor gangster who worked for the notorious Kray twins.[6] Whitehead was known for knocking his girls around, which would explain why Rees had left him in late September. The word on the street was that Whitehead was looking for her to teach her a lesson. That avenue fizzled out though. Whitehead was the obvious suspect but there was no evidence to tie him to her death, and as an associate of the famously violent Krays he was

---

6 TruTV Crime Library, Jack The Stripper: Death of a Good Time Girl
    http://www.trutv.com/library/crime/serial_killers/unsolved/jack_the_stripper/2.html

protected by a wall of silence. Plenty of people would be willing to give him an alibi; none would inform on him. If he'd strangled Rees he was probably going to get away with it.

Some of the detectives were wondering, though. Over four years earlier but barely a mile away the body of 21-year-old Elizabeth Figg, also known as Ann Phillips, had been found propped against a tree. Marks round her neck showed that she had been strangled, and her dress had been ripped away from her upper body to leave her breasts hanging out. Figg was another runaway who'd drifted to London, this time from the north of England, and like Rees she'd had a violent ponce. Fenton "Baby" Ward, a former boxer from Trinidad, had quickly been picked up and questioned by the police but ruled out as a suspect. The Met had no doubt he was a violent thug and fully capable of killing if it suited him, but they just didn't see him having killed Figg. The murder had puzzled them at the time and disquiet lingered. Yes, prostitutes got killed, but it wasn't normal for their bodies to be so publicly dumped.

In the late 1950s and early 60s social attitudes were very different from today, and the death of a prostitute attracted a lot less attention than the murder of a "respectable" woman would have done. There would be no press outrage, no local campaigns to find the killer. The police took it seriously enough, though. They weren't going to get much help from other prostitutes – many of whom, in an era of routine arrests for "soliciting," had no reason to love the police – but the idea of a killer stalking the city's vice scene troubled some of them. Tarts died; sometimes it was an angry customer, sometimes a violent pimp, sometimes just their bad luck at being out on the streets alone and vulnerable. Rees's death was the latest on a long, unhappy list. Still, it was unusual enough that some of the detectives made a mental note, just in case something similar happened again. They wouldn't have long to wait. Four years had passed since the death of Elizabeth Figg, but things were about to speed up dramatically. In a few short months the sight of a stripped and strangled corpse was going to become very familiar to the luckless members of the Murder Squad.

[2]

FEAR IN LONDON

Hammersmith Bridge has been taking traffic across the Thames since 1887. The 700 foot long structure has survived two World Wars and three terrorist bombs, and now it's prized by architects as one of the country's finest Victorian iron bridges. It's also a popular place for rowers and boaters, including the London Corinthians Sailing Club. Corinthians members like to sail dinghies on the river, and some of them are dedicated enough to get out on the water in all sorts of weather. February 2, 1964 was dry and warm for that time of year – over 53°F – and some of the Corinthians took advantage of it to cruise down to Hammersmith. Near the bridge one of the crews had their outing abruptly ruined. Wedged against a floating pontoon moored to the bank was something that looked suspiciously like a body. The sailors eased off the sheets, slowed and cautiously turned in to have a closer look. Sure enough, a bloated corpse was snagged against the pontoon.7 Spend any amount of time on the Thames in a small boat and you'll see all sorts of things floating by, but the nude body of a woman isn't one you're going to meet every day.

An autopsy found water in the dead woman's lungs, meaning she had probably died of drowning. That happens often enough – about 450 people a year accidentally drown in Britain – but the police were pretty sure this wasn't an accident. The woman had been stripped almost naked before she went in the water, leaving only a pair of stockings pulled down around her ankles. Some of her teeth had been knocked out and her stained underwear

7 Crimetime.co.uk, Cathi Unsworth on Bad Penny Blues
http://www.crimetime.co.uk/community/mag.php/showcomments/1406

was crammed into her mouth. There were also marks that suggested she'd been at least partially strangled. The nudity and missing teeth hinted at a connection to Rees. When the body was identified as 30-year-old prostitute Hanna Tailford definite warning flags were raised.

Tailford had last been seen alive on January 24, and according to the pathologists the state of her body made it likely she'd been in the river for a week. That isn't actually a surprising length of time for a corpse to go undiscovered; the Thames in London is a busy river, but there's no shortage of places for a cadaver to float out of sight. Until tides or currents pull it out into the open there's no guarantee anybody will see it. Tailford could even have been under the pontoon since her death, just waiting for someone to sail close by in a low, open boat.

Like the first two victims Tailford had run away from home as a teenager, unable to settle in the northern mining town where she'd been brought up. In London she soon ended up on the streets. Selling herself hadn't always brought in enough money to live, and her long record of soliciting convictions was livened up by a few for theft. Once, pregnant, she even tried to sell the unborn child through a newspaper ad.8 There was more to her career than a desperate struggle for cash, though. Difficult as it was to get information from the other hookers, the Met Police slowly built up a picture of a life lived on the border between the sleaze of street vice and the big money of London's social scene. Tailford hadn't just been a prostitute, it turned out. She'd also been involved in the pornographic movie industry, and had been paid to entertain at society parties.

On April 8 Irene Lockwood, 26 years old, was found on a narrow mud beach only 300 yards upriver from where Tailford's corpse had been discovered. Lockwood had been alive the day before, loitering outside a pub in Chiswick.

---

8 TruTV Crime Library, Jack The Stripper:A Scandalous Death?
http://www.trutv.com/library/crime/serial_killers/unsolved/jack_the_stripper/3.html

Now she'd been stripped, strangled – probably with her own underwear - and thrown in the river. The autopsy found that she'd been four months pregnant and inquiries among other girls soon revealed that she, like Rees, had been trying to get an abortion. This time there was no wondering if her death had been the result of an abortion gone wrong; Lockwood had clearly been murdered.

It wouldn't be hard to find someone who wanted Irene Lockwood dead. She was a notorious scam artist, who specialized in persuading clients to take their trousers off outside her bedroom so an accomplice could go through their pockets while she had sex with them. She'd also been involved in illegal late night card games that had left a lot of gamblers with a nasty feeling that they'd been cheated. (which they had.) There was a long list of people who hated her and her death, normally, wouldn't have been seen as all that surprising. In fact a friend of hers had been beaten to death in 1963 by a client she'd tried to blackmail with explicit photographs. Boosting your income through theft and blackmail depends on a steady supply of victims who're more frightened of embarrassment than they are of getting their hands dirty, and a misjudgment can be dangerous.

The police were spotting some disturbing similarities to the previous killings, though. Like Figg, Rees and Tailford, Lockwood was short – only five feet two. Rees and Tailford had also been pregnant and all four women had dark hair. (although Lockwood's was dyed blonde.) All four had suffered from sexually transmitted diseases during their careers in the sex trade. Three of them had been found along the same stretch of river in the space of five months. This was enough to make the cluster of killings stand out from the routine attrition of London's streetwalkers. It looked increasingly as if a serial killer was stalking hookers along the Thames in west London.

Once Lockwood was identified the police began taking her life apart searching for clues. Her diary referred to a man called "Kenny," and that looked like it might be a lead. Lockwood's gambling scam had been set up by Kenneth Archibald, the caretaker at Holland Park Tennis Club. Tennis clubs have an image as respectable organizations, and this one was – during the day. At night it was a bit different. At the time Britain had some of the strictest drinking laws in Europe and an evening out would be ended by the familiar 10:45pm call of "last orders please." That didn't suit everyone so in large cities there were always illegal drinking dens if you looked hard enough. These were often in private homes or lock-up garages, but Archibald went one better than that. His job put him in charge of a clubhouse with a fully equipped bar, and as long as it was in good shape during official opening hours there was nothing to stop him exploiting it. Operating by word of mouth Archibald turned the club into an illicit party venue, and it attracted a collection of shady characters. Late-night drinkers mingled with prostitutes and thrill seekers, and the club grounds and tennis courts provided plenty of secluded corners for sex. Lockwood was one of the hookers who frequented the club.

There was nothing to link Archibald to the earlier victims but now he was flagged as a potential suspect. If he knew Lockwood then he had at least some association with the vice scene, so it was feasible that he knew or had at least met the other dead women. If he'd trusted Lockwood enough to make her a partner in a lucrative racket then his links with hookers obviously went a bit further than a quick fumble in some alley, too. The Met decided that Kenneth Archibald was somebody they'd like to speak to. The 57-year-old was interviewed, but denied knowing Lockwood at all despite her having his phone number on a card in her apartment.   Then for some reason his story changed dramatically; on April 27 he walked into Notting Hill police station and asked to speak to a detective. He'd changed his mind, Archibald told the astonished desk sergeant; he'd killed her and he wanted to confess.

It seemed that the killings might have been solved almost as soon as the presence of a serial killer had been identified. In many ways Archibald looked good as a suspect. He'd already been on the Met's radar because of his links with Lockwood. Now he told the Notting Hill cops how Lockwood had been killed, and when and where he'd thrown her body into the river. He'd met her outside the Chiswick pub, he said, then later argued with her about money and strangled her in a rage. His story wasn't perfect but the basics were a close enough match to the facts of the case. Archibald was charged with murder and detained. Not everyone was convinced though. Archibald was in poor health and had mental health issues – always a red flag when someone confesses to a murder. At his trial in June he changed his mind again, retracted his confession and said he'd made the whole thing up while depressed. The jury agreed and he was acquitted of Lockwood's murder. It's fairly certain that was the right decision, because the Stripper killings hadn't stopped with his arrest.

With two definite victims of a serial killer and two more possible the police had been

taking steps to catch the killer in the act. All
four bodies had been found in and around the
Thames. Now patrols around the river were increased. If the killer was picking off his victims
near the river the extra activity might deter
him; if he was just dumping them there then
better surveillance increased the chances of
catching him in the act. The police were about
to be disappointed on both counts.

Helen Barthelemy was a former circus per-
former from Blackpool, although her parents
were French and Scottish. Aged 20, she had a
criminal record in her home town from before
she'd moved to London – she had been con-
victed of luring a man to a quiet spot with
promises of sex, but instead he'd been slashed
with a razor then robbed. Now Barthelemy herself had apparently been lured away and at-
tacked. She had last been seen in a bar by one
of her friends; Barthelemy had left her handbag
there, saying she was just going out for a short
while. She never came back. On April 24 –
three days before Archibald's confession – her
naked body was found in a lane near a sports

field in Brentwood. This was a change in the pattern; her corpse was dumped well to the northwest of the earlier victims, and over a mile from the river. There was no doubt that she'd fallen victim to the same killer though. As well as the now familiar marks of ligature strangulation and the removal of her clothes she was a small, dark haired street prostitute who'd suffered from an STD.

As well as the similarities with the previous murders there were some new and interesting things about this corpse. Barthelemy's body was filthy, suggesting that it had been stored somewhere for a while between being stripped and dumped. Close examination of her skin also found thousands of tiny particles of paint. This was the type used for spraying cars and other metal objects and the microscopic flecks were in a rainbow of colors. The detectives suspected that she had been stored near a workshop where spraying was going on, and airborne paint particles had found their way into the improvised crypt and onto her skin. This didn't immediately pinpoint the place where the body had been kept – London has hundreds of small paint shops and light industrial premises – but it was something.

Now something else was suggested, too. Following Barthelemy's discovery a new detective joined the team, Detective Superintendent William Baldock. Baldock questioned the assumption that the victims had been strangled, and instead suggested something startling and horrifying. Many of the women had teeth knocked out, he said. Perhaps they'd been asphyxiated while performing oral sex and these weren't deliberate murders, but a deviant sex act gone wrong. Because fellatio was much more of a taboo subject than it is today this idea appalled many people. Could there be any truth in it? Not likely. A moment's thought suggests that any prostitute in this position had a simple way to resist – bite, hard. All of them still had enough teeth left to make the point quickly and brutally. Baldock's suggestion hit hard at the time but today it's really just a sign of how prudish people were only a couple of

generations ago. If it wasn't in such a grim con-
text it would even be amusing.

Other police suggestions were more helpful.
Baldock wasn't the only new member of the
team – the head of Scotland Yard Criminal Investigation Department, Commander George
Hatherill, had now taken over the investigation.
Hatherill knew the best source of information
on the dead women was their fellow prostitutes and it was essential to break down the
barrier of trust that kept them away from the
police. In an attempt to do this he took a bold
step – he publicly appealed for prostitutes to
come forward, under a promise of anonymity, if
they knew anything that might help. Hatherill
pointed out that if the Stripper wasn't stopped
it would be prostitutes who would die. If anyone had been forced to strip by a client, or assaulted by one, they should contact the Met
immediately. It worked – to a point. Hatherill's
appeal was made on April 28 and two days later 45 prostitutes – and 25 men – had supplied
information. None of it pinpointed the Stripper's identity though, and Hatherill's warning

about the risk to hookers was about to be
proven accurate.

Just after five in the morning on July 14 a
chauffeur, up early to get his car ready, found
Mary Fleming's body propped against a garage
door in a street in Chiswick. Like Barthelemy
this corpse was over a mile from the Thames,
this time to the north of the first discoveries.
Fleming, a tough 30-year-old Glaswegian
who'd been on the streets for a decade, was
well known for taking no nonsense from difficult clients and would fight back savagely if
threatened. She might have been small but she
carried a knife and she'd used it before. If
she'd pulled it this time it hadn't helped her.
The evidence collected from her nude remains
suggested she'd put up a struggle, but her as-
sailant had stunned her with a powerful blow
over the heart then strangled her. This time the
pathologist was careful to examine her skin,
looking for traces of paint. He found them.
Fleming's body had spent time in the same
place as the previous victim. There could be
absolutely no doubt that they were the work of

the same predator. Inquiries around the site of the gruesome discovery suggested that the chauffeur had barely missed getting a sight of the Stripper's vehicle – neighbors had heard a car reversing down the street minutes before he found the body.

The location where Fleming's body was dumped showed another change in tactics by the murderer. When the police had increased patrols around the river he had outsmarted them by leaving Barthelemy well to the north. That was enough to leave some people wondering how he had predicted the police response, and even to wonder if he had inside knowledge of what the Met were doing – speculation that would resurface years later when possible suspects were discussed. By leaving her where he did it was as if he was saying "I know how you're trying to catch me, and it won't work." There was a heavy police presence in Chiswick, though. Most of the detectives felt this was a deliberate taunt. It all added to the pressure. By now over 8,000 people had been interviewed in connection with the case and the press were calling for an arrest before anyone else died. The tabloids had also given the killer his nickname – "Jack the Stripper" was in the headlines.

The paint flecks were the final clue the police needed to announce that all the murders were the work of one man. If the same traces had been found on the earlier victims it would have confirmed that fact sooner, but it's probably not too surprising that nothing showed up. Figg is perhaps the most likely of the eight to have been killed by someone else; she died four years before the next victim and was the only one who wasn't found naked. If she were a victim of the Stripper he would have been developing his methods at the time. Why did he start stripping the bodies? The victims were unlikely to have undressed themselves – they were streetwalkers who did the "car trade." At the time a lot of their business was oral sex – which "nice girls" wouldn't do – and even if a client wanted full sex they would just lift their skirt and pull down their panties. No, the clothes had been removed by the killer. The chances are that it was to eliminate evidence. Perhaps he'd left semen on their clothes, and while DNA matching was unknown at the time it might have been possible to match blood groups. Clothing also picks up fibers and hair, and even in 1964 detectives could do a lot with evidence like that; the main tool used to analyze them is a microscope, and unlike DNA sequencing microscopes have been around for centuries. It makes sense that the Stripper would have removed the clothing before storing the bodies, as that reduced the chances of the police collecting evidence from where the bodies were found. Of course it also let paint settle on the skin, but the tiny droplets would have formed a thin, invisible mist in the air and it would take a very smart killer to think of that. The paint on the skin wasn't obvious; it took good forensic work to find it on Bathelemy and the later victims. If Rees was killed by the Stripper and stored in the same place it would have been difficult to find the clue after she'd spent weeks buried in a pile of garbage. Tailford and Lockwood had been thrown in a polluted river, and in Tailford's case she'd been in the water for a week. Water and decay would have removed a lot of the paint. It was only when the Stripper altered his methods and started abandoning corpses on dry land that the clue started to show up. It would soon show up again.

On October 23 Kim Taylor was working with her friend Frances Brown, also known as Margaret McGowan, near a pub in Notting Hill. Events of the last months had made them wary; like Mary Fleming and many other girls they were carrying knives or sharpened steel combs, but obviously that wasn't enough to guarantee a girl's safety. Taylor and Brown had decided to work as a pair for safety; that way, they figured, the Stripper wouldn't be able to pick them off. They'd been joking earlier in the pub about the chances of meeting the killer, but they both knew it wasn't a laughing matter. Back outside they were watching over each other, casting suspicious glances at any man who approached to talk.

When two cars pulled up at the same time both girls took a good look at the one the other was getting into. Brown climbed into a Ford, either a Zodiac or a Zephyr, and Taylor got into the other car. The vehicles soon split up in the London traffic. Taylor did what her client paid her to do, returned to the pub and waited for Brown to return. She never did.

It was over a month before Taylor found out what had happened to her friend. On November 25 Brown's body was found in Horton Street, Kensington, just outside an underground Civil Defense building. Unlike the other bodies, which were left in plain sight, Brown's had been partly concealed; dead branches and a dustbin lid had been piled on the corpse. Apart from that anomaly the marks of the Stripper were clear. She had been strangled and undressed, and her body was speckled with tiny particles of colored paint. She was also a short, dark-haired prostitute with a history of STD infection, but the nudity and paint settled it anyway. The Stripper had killed another one.

This time it wasn't just the victim's clothes that were missing. Some of Brown's jewelry was gone as well. When she vanished she had been wearing a gold ring and a silver cross on a chain, but these had vanished. They weren't the sort of items that would hold much evidence, and in fact they were risky things for the killer to have taken – they were identifiable, and if he'd been caught with them in his possession he would have had a hard time explaining how he came to have them. Stealing them was a risk that seemed out of character for the usually meticulous Stripper.

The first time most people heard about psychological profiling of serial killers was from the 1991 movie The Silence of the Lambs, but as a technique it's been in use since the 1940s. Scotland Yard were busily trying to build one for the Stripper. Police psychologists suggested that Brown's missing jewelry meant he might be collecting souvenirs from his victims. They also believed he was probably a shy man who seemed outwardly quiet. The small size of all the victims – none was taller than five feet two inches – suggested that he was small himself and chose targets he could easily overpower. Some of what the psychologists said could be useful in building a case once the Stripper was in custody, but it didn't do a lot towards finding him. Before a profile can be used to narrow down a list of suspects there has to be a list to work with, and the pool of men who might be the Stripper was huge. If anything Brown's death made it larger.

[3]

THE PLOT THICKENS

The psychologists had been looking at the case from a purely criminal angle – that a madman was stalking and killing streetwalkers for some demented reason of his own. Brown's death raised a new possibility. The latest victim had a link with Hanna Tailford that brought the two of them onto the fringes – and maybe much deeper – of a major Establishment scandal. It wasn't hard to imagine that events at the highest levels of the British government had driven someone to hunt down and kill the two hookers to keep them quiet. An officially sanctioned assassin might have used the Stripper murders as cover or killed the other girls to disguise his true targets. There might even have been some common factor about the victims that made them all targets. In fact that wasn't all that unlikely. All five of the women killed in 1964 lived – and often worked – in Ladbroke Grove, an area to the west of Kensington that's named for the main road running through it. It also borders Notting Hill, where Frances Brown had picked up her last lethal client. Perhaps, like Brown, they had some link to a controversy that eventually brought down Harold Macmillan's Conservative government.

On December 14, 1962 Johnny Edgecombe, a drifter and small-time dope dealer from Antigua, turned up at the apartment of a leading London doctor and tried to shoot through the lock on the front door. He was trying to get in to speak to his ex-girlfriend, call girl Christine Keeler. The Met Police don't appreciate gunplay much, though, and Edgecombe was arrested. Three months later, when Keeler failed to appear to give evidence at his trial, one of the biggest scandals of the 1960s exploded in the British press.

Keeler had been in a relationship with Edgecombe, but that hadn't been enough for her. She'd also been going around with Aloysius "Lucky" Gordon, a vicious Jamaican thug who'd once held her hostage for two days and threatened her with an ax. Edgecombe had already got into a fight with Gordon and slashed his face. That wasn't what the press were interested in though. One of her gentleman friends was John Profumo, the Secretary of State for War. What made it a matter of some concern was that another was a Soviet spy.

Profumo had been introduced to Keeler by Stephen Ward, the fashionable doctor whose apartment door Edgecombe had shot up. Ward was known for introducing friends – and he had many – to girls, including high-class prostitutes like Keeler and Mandy Rice-Davies. When the Profumo affair hit the newspapers Ward was arrested and charged with living on immoral earnings. He was tried in July 1963 and a string of prostitutes were called to give evidence. Among them were Hannah Tailford and Frances Brown. On July 31 Ward was cleared of "procuring" prostitutes – pimping – but found guilty on the immoral earnings charges. He wasn't in court to hear the verdict; he was in hospital in a coma, induced by an overdose of sleeping pills the day before. He died on August 3 without regaining consciousness.

It's likely Ward took an overdose after hearing what the prosecuting counsel had to say about him – he swallowed the pills within hours of the prosecution's unflattering summary – but because the case reached so far into the government it was inevitable there would be speculation. Had Ward been silenced to preserve the reputations of powerful men? His fashionable parties had attracted the cream of British society, and he'd been on the boundary between that society and the violent cesspit of the London underworld. Tailford had talked of being hired to go to a party in 1960, and being taken to a large house in up-market Eaton Square. She'd ended up performing a floor show with a man in a gorilla suit.[9] Tailford had

9 Crimetime.co.uk, Cathi Unsworth on Bad Penny Blues
http://www.crimetime.co.uk/community/mag.php/showcomments/1406

also taken part in pornographic movies, made in an apartment in the seedy streets around Victoria station. Her association with Ward showed that Brown was also on that murky boundary and it wasn't incredible to think that she'd seen or heard something that made her a target.

Of course if it was an MI5 hit man who'd killed Brown he'd been surprisingly careless in letting Taylor get a good look at him. After Brown's body was discovered Taylor spoke to a police artist and a sketch of the suspect was produced. It showed a stocky man of medium height, with a round face. The case had now taken on a much higher profile than before; the murders of a couple of hookers might not attract much public attention, but the existence of a serial killer was a different matter. Before any leads emerged, though, the Stripper struck again.

Brigit "Bridie" O'Hara was a 28-year-old Irish woman living in Shepherd's Bush with her husband and children. None of her neighbors knew that she moonlighted as a prostitute to top up the family's income. Unlike the previous Stripper victims she worked alone, and didn't have any connections to the underground party scene. On January 11, 1965 O'Hara was seen with three men near the Holland Park underground station. That was also where Elizabeth Figg had last been seen. Two of the men had Welsh accents. The third was described as an older man. O'Hara was never seen alive again.

On February 16 O'Hara's body was found on the Heron Trading Estate in Acton, about a mile and a half north of where Fleming had been dumped. She had been strangled or choked to death, several of her teeth had been knocked out and her nude body was flecked with paint. The autopsy also suggested that her corpse had been stored somewhere warm for a while before being brought out and left behind a shed – although she'd been missing for over a month the corpse wasn't decayed, and in fact had been partly mummified.

Scotland Yard's response to the latest murder was to appoint a new chief to the investigation. Detective Chief Superintendent John

Du Rose, the head of the Murder Squad, was on vacation, but the Met called him back to take charge. Du Rose was nicknamed "Four Day Johnny" thanks to the speed with which he'd solved previous murder cases. He was known as an active and innovative detective, and he quickly expanded the search for the Stripper. Police started logging the details of every car they saw after dark in a large area of west London. Any car "kerb crawling" for prostitutes was recorded on a separate list and police called on the drivers to interview them. There weren't many female detectives in the 1960s but young, attractive policewomen were drafted in, dressed up in miniskirts and high heels and sent out to totter around the red light areas. Any man who approached them with a proposition would be shown a warrant card and then interrogated. Real streetwalkers complained that it was harming their business but Du Rose had other concerns. He wanted the killer, and among other things that meant finding where the bodies had been stored.

Hundreds of policemen started visiting light manufacturing companies and automobile spray shops throughout west London. Examination of the traces found on the bodies had pinpointed the exact brands of paint they were looking for, and every spraying facility in a 24 square mile area was examined to see if it used the critical combination of paints. Finally one was found on the Heron Trading Estate, yards from where O'Hara's body had been dumped. Opposite the workshop was an electricity substation, a small gated compound with a bank of transformers in it. A cable ran in to this from a main grid pylon and was stepped down to 240 volt and 440 volt currents[10] for distribution to surrounding homes and businesses. The cables taking power to the local area were buried, and at the substation they ran in crawl spaces covered by boards. Detectives searched in the crawl spaces and found a film of paint flecks that exactly matched what had been found on the Stripper's victims. The crawl spaces were

---

[10] In the UK domestic electricity is at 240 volts. Most homes also have a three phase, 440 volt supply for electric cookers, and many light industries use three-phase supplies.

also warm, heated by the power flowing through the cables. This was where the bodies had been kept before being scattered across the city. With a location haunted by the Stripper now definitely identified the police felt that real progress had been made. They interviewed thousands of people who worked on the trading estate or lived nearby. Vehicles were searched. Du Rose announced that the list of suspects had been narrowed down to three people, and would soon be reduced to one. But no arrest was ever made, and the Stripper never killed again. As months passed with no more nude bodies the prostitutes – and the police – slowly started to believe that the reign of terror was over. The mystery was as impenetrable as ever.

[4]

WHO WAS THE STRIPPER?

With the killings at an end the story of Jack the Stripper slowly faded from the media. When people thought of it they mostly felt that the police had failed to catch a serial killer – the most prolific in the UK up to that point – who'd been operating right under their noses. In 1970 John Du Rose, by then retired, claimed that this wasn't true; Scotland Yard had been on the point of arresting the Stripper when he'd killed himself. This claim was repeated in Du Rose's autobiography, then in Brian McConnell's 1974 book Found Naked and Dead. But was it true? Who were the suspects in the Stripper case and what was the evidence against them? In fact there were more than three, and while they all have intriguing links to the murders none of them are a perfect fit. The fact is every name

that's been put forward is based on speculation, guesswork and sometimes a healthy dose
of imagination. The Stripper could be any one
of the men on that list or he could have been
someone entirely different, someone that was
never even suspected of the crimes.

Mungo Ireland

Mungo "Jock" Ireland was brought up by a
strictly religious family in Scotland; his child-
hood was marked by frequent lectures about
sin and equally frequent beatings when his be-
havior disappointed his devout parents. He'd
served in the military during the Second World
War and had allegedly picked up a habit of us-
ing prostitutes. He also started drinking and
revealed a violent streak. After the war he
joined the police, but was turned down for a
transfer to the detective branch and quit in

disgust.11 Finally he started working as a security guard. In 1964 he had a job on the Heron Trading Estate, and he had keys for the electricity substation.

Du Rose never named his main suspect, but later researchers identified Ireland through the circumstances of his death. In March 1965 he parked his car in a lockup garage, ran a hose in the window and killed himself by carbon monoxide poisoning. His wife found a note on the kitchen table at their home in Putney. It read:

> *I can't stick it any longer. It may be my fault but not all of it. I'm sorry Harry is a burden to you. Give my love to the kid. Farewell, Jock. PS. To save you and the*

---

11 TruTV Crime Library, Jack The Stripper:"Big John"
http://www.trutv.com/library/crime/serial_killers/unsolved/jack_the_stripper/11.html

*police looking for me I'll be in the
garage.*

At first glance that looks like strong evidence for Ireland's guilt. He was clearly admitting guilt for something, and expected the police to come looking for him. Was he admitting to the Stripper murders and in fear of a knock on the door from Du Rose and the murder squad? Maybe. Or maybe not. Ireland's marriage was in trouble, which could be both a reason for suicide and what he was taking responsibility for. He was also due in court for a motoring offence, which would explain why he'd been concerned about the police. And while he had been employed at the Heron Trading Estate he'd only been working there for three weeks when he killed himself; when Bridie O'Hara's body was dumped he'd been back home in Scotland.

Freddie Mills

Freddie Mills was born in Bournemouth, Hampshire in 1919. As a teenager be began fighting in fairground booths and started boxing as a light heavyweight in 1936. Known for his fast, aggressive punching, he took the British and Commonwealth light heavyweight title in 1942, the European title at the same weight in 1947 and in 1948 he defeated American Gus Lesnevich to take the world title. He lost it in 1950 to another American fighter, Joey Maxim, and retired weeks later.

In retirement Mills became a TV personality, and also opened a nightclub in central London's Soho district. He became friendly with the Kray twins – who had both fought semi-professionally as teenagers - and taught boxing to local youths. By the early 1960s, however, the nightclub was beginning to struggle and Mills ran into serious financial problems. In July 1965 he climbed into his car behind the nightclub and shot himself in the head with a borrowed rifle.12 In 2001 rumors began that he had killed himself because he believed the police were about to arrest him for the Stripper killings.

Where did these rumors come from? Some of them appear to be based on off the record interviews with other prominent boxers of the time. Another possible source is the descriptions of the main suspect leaked by Du Rose and other policemen. Du Rose had said that the killer was a married man in his 40s, which certainly described Mills but also fitted Mungo Ireland perfectly. Other whispers from inside the Met mentioned that he had boxed and it looks like that may have brought Mills into the frame. The investigation into the boxer's death was led by Scotland Yard detective Leonard "Nipper" Read, who later became famous for bringing down the Kray empire. Read rejects

---

12 Some sources say he shot himself twice, which has raised questions about the verdict of suicide.

Mills as a Stripper suspect. 13 It seems likely that Read is right, and that Mills has only become associated with the case through confused release of information.

Tommy Butler

Tommy Butler is an unusual candidate to be suspected of serial murder. At the time of the Stripper killings he was a Superintendent in the Metropolitan Police Flying Squad, a specialist unit responsible for investigating and preventing armed robberies. Butler was named as a potential suspect in a 2001 book, The Survivor, and the idea has gained some popularity from there. However The Survivor was the autobiography of Jimmy Evans, a former criminal who specialized in blowing safes and was linked to

---

13 The Guardian, November 4, 2001, Boxing hero Freddie Mills ,murdered eight women,' Tony Thompson
      http://www.theguardian.com/uk/2001/nov/04/sport.tonythompson

the Kray gang. Neither Evans nor his ghost-writer had any inside knowledge of the case and it has been suggested – convincingly – that Evans simply named a senior Flying Squad officer he had a personal grudge against. After all the Flying Squad made its name arresting robbers, and Evans was a robber. It's believed he had several encounters with Butler and hated him as a result.

It's suggestive that nobody ever suggested Butler as a suspect while he was alive to defend himself. No actual evidence has ever been put forward to back up the accusation, and most people with a serious interest in the case don't think much of Evans's allegation.

Andrew Cushway

Andrew John Cushway was another police officer, a Detective Constable with the Met. He has been fingered as a suspect mostly because of clues given in the 2006 book Jack of Jumps. It's believed this theory came from Detective Superintendent William Baldock - the oral sex expert - who investigated Cushway's original crimes in 1962. The reasoning behind this seems to be that he was dismissed in disgrace in 1962 after being caught committing a series of burglaries. The motivation for Cushway's crimes was to make colleagues he didn't get on with look bad, and the book seems to be based on the assumption that after serving jail time for the robberies he went on to kill eight women for the same reason. It's not really very convincing and Cushway has never been seen as a credible suspect. Baldock himself predicted that if Cushway was actually the Stripper he would kill again after O'Hara's murder.[14] Of course O'Hara was the last victim in the string. Cushway was also a spectacularly inept criminal. He couldn't even carry out a few simple burglaries without quickly getting caught, so it seems unlikely he could have pulled off eight

---

14 Everything2, Jack the Stripper
http://everything2.com/title/Jack+the+Stripper

elaborate murders without leaving a single piece of evidence that pointed to himself.

Kenneth Archibald

Kenneth Archibald, the tennis club caretaker who confessed to killing Irene Lockwood, has to be included in any list of suspects. Of course it's impossible for him to have committed all the murders, but in theory he could have been responsible for Lockwood's death. Had he heard about Tailford's death and decided to use it as cover to get rid of a potentially dangerous business partner? It's possible – but not very likely. Archibald was known to have mental health problems and when confessions are involved that's always a red flag. His physical health was also poor. Lockwood was a small woman, but she was a lot younger and stronger than Archibald and unless she was drugged – which the autopsy showed no trace of – he would have had a hard time subduing and strangling her.

Harold Jones

And then of course there's Harold Jones, the Abertillery shop assistant who murdered two young girls in 1921. Jones was first nominated as a Stripper suspect in May 2011 by the Crime and Investigation Network's Murder Casebook show.15 The same month Welsh author Neil Milkins published a book, Who was Jack the Stripper? exploring the possibility of Evans as the Stripper in more depth.

By some definitions Jones was already a serial killer before he was sent to jail. The FBI class serial killing as "a series of two or more murders, committed as separate events, usually, but not always, by one offender acting alone" and that means Jones qualifies. Many serial killers, whether or not they're finally detected, stop killing naturally. Jones didn't; he was ar-

---

15 Talent Television, Fred Dinenage: Murder Casebook
http://www.talenttv.com/productions/casebook/casebook.php

rested within days of his second murder and spent the next 20 years in prison. He was released in 1941 against the recommendations of the governor and prison psychiatrist, apparently to give him a chance to redeem himself by enlisting in the armed forces. Instead he vanished. His final incarceration was at Wandsworth Prison in southwest London.

If Jones was still dangerous when released – as the Wandsworth psychiatrist believed he was – it seems unlikely that he would wait until 1959 before killing again. Of course it's always possible that he didn't. There are no records of his movements between his release and 1948, but he occasionally returned to Abertillery after the war to visit his parents[16] – and possibly the graves of his first victims. If he returned to Wales, did he also kill there again? In June

16 Wales Online, Nov 25, 2007, Author names new killer in Drinkwater case

http://www.walesonline.co.uk/news/wales-news/author-names-new-killer-drinkwater-2220319

1946 12-year-old Muriel Drinkwater, from Penl-
lergaer near Swansea, was abducted as she
walked home after school. She was taken to a
nearby wood, raped and then shot through the
heart with a .45 caliber Colt M1909 revolver.

Neil Milkins believes that Jones may have
killed Muriel Drinkwater. Does that also mean
he could have been the Stripper? It could be
argued that the Welsh murders were very different from the later London series. Drinkwater
was raped, as Freda Buenell had been in 1921,
but there was probably no sexual element in
the Stripper killings. There are a few other hints
that could point to Jones, though.

The UK electoral register was suspended
during the Second World War so there is no
clue as to where Jones was in the years following his release. He next surfaced in 1948 under
the name of Harry Stevens, living in a room at
29 Hestercombe Avenue, Fulham. This street of
red brick row houses is a typical pre-War lower
middle class London residential area, and at
first sight it seems an odd place to find someone like Jones. The war left tens of thousands

of middle-aged widows in London, however, and many of them had financial problems. For decades afterwards thousands of them supplemented their income by taking in lodgers or even turning their homes into rooming houses for the workers who flooded in to rebuild the battered capital.

Jones lived in Herstercombe Avenue for 14 years, then in 1962 he dropped out of sight again. This time he was off the radar for four years before turning up again, under the name Harry Jones, at 51 Aldensley road. Aldensley Road is a similar area, once dotted with rooming houses, and it's less than two miles to the north of Hestercombe Avenue. Where was Jones in the meantime? He seems to have felt at home in Fulham, so perhaps he was somewhere else in the area under a different name. What may be significant is that during the period Jones was unaccounted for all but one of the Stripper murders took place. Was Jones somewhere in Fulham, picking off easy targets from the surrounding area to satiate the voices in his head that told him to kill? It's certainly possible, and there's an intriguing clue. Bridie O'Hara was last seen on January 11, 1965. That was Harold Jones's 59th birthday. Was he the older man she was seen with that night, perhaps out celebrating with a couple of fellow Welshmen? Was O'Hara's murder a gruesome gift to himself?

Jones died of cancer in 1971; the death certificate listed his occupation as "night watchman." Now, private security staff are often students or low-income workers supplementing their main wage. In 1960s Britain it was a bit different. Many watchmen were ex-soldiers like Mungo Ireland, men of similar age to Jones. It's a job that would have given Jones the opportunities he needed to carry out the killings. Did he ever work at the Heron Trading Estate? So many employment records have been lost that it's impossible to say, especially as we know that Jones used different names.

It's unlikely that DNA samples could be recovered from any of the victims and Jones's body was cremated in 1971, so even if he was the Stripper hard evidence will probably never be found. It's definitely possible he was, though. The evidence pointing to him is circumstantial and to some extent based on coincidences. Maybe the strongest point is that O'Hara was killed on his birthday and one of her last contacts was a man who could have been Jones.

Two Killers?

Because Jones is most strongly linked to the O'Hara murder it's been suggested that he could have worked with Ireland to kill the women. This would also explain Ireland's absence when O'Hara's body was dumped – Jones moved the body alone. Is this a credible explanation? It's not impossible. Ireland had a violent streak and if he and Jones had ever worked together – of course that's unknown – they could have been drawn to each other's flaws. They lived quite close together. Fulham and Putney face each other across the Thames, so it's not out of the question that they knew each other. On the other hand there's no evidence that they did.

An Unsolvable Mystery

Nearly fifty years have passed since the Stripper last killed. By now it's unlikely that he is still alive. The list of suspects is a varied one, with some names on it for good reason and others apparently there out of spite or speculation. The chances of finding physical evidence to link anybody to the murders is remote. Unless somebody makes a deathbed confession or the jewelry stolen from some of the victims turns up when a house is being cleared the crimes will probably never be solved. That makes the mystery all the more interesting, but it has a human cost as well. Several of the victims had children who are still alive; it might help them to know that their mothers' killer had at least been identified even if the chances of him being punished are remote.

[5]

THE LEGACY OF A MADMAN

Britain has had its fair share of serial killers over the years and many of them are household names. The infamous doctor Harold Shipman was the most prolific British murderer of the 20th century, and is very likely the most lethal in the world; he was jailed in 2000 for murdering 15 of his patients by giving them lethal injections, but it's almost certain he killed a further 218 people and the total number of his victims is unknown. It's believed to be at least 250 and could be many more – during his career 459 people died under his care. Fred and Rosemary West buried eleven girls and young women under their patio, and before his 1995 suicide Fred told a prison visitor that he'd killed at least 20 more. Dennis Nilsen killed eleven young men between 1978 and 1983, washing and dressing their corpses and keeping them in his apartment for company until they began to smell and had to be replaced with fresh ones. Peter Sutcliffe, the Yorkshire Ripper, started out killing prostitutes after one stole £10 from him – although he claimed that God told him to do it - and later began killing women at random; his total victims numbered 13. By the grim score applied to their kind these four were the worst British serial killers of the 20th century and they're all nearly as notorious today as they were when they were arrested.

What's remarkable is that Jack the Stripper, who comes in at number five when the century's murderous tally is taken, has been almost forgotten by comparison. The Moors Murderers, Ian Brady and Myra Hindley, murdered five but are much better known. Why is the Stripper so low profile compared to other, more famous cases? A large part of it is probably the fact that nobody was ever arrested. Arrest, trial and tabloid stories about love-struck prison visitors, hunger strikes and new identities all help to keep a case in the news. His choice of victims must have a lot to do with it as well. Attitudes have changed a lot since the 1960s but there are still many people who, when a prostitute gets murdered, think she must have been asking for it in some way. Rightly or wrongly, a dead sex worker is a lot less likely to attract public outrage than a murdered child.

The Stripper and his victims haven't completely faded into the mists of history, however. Interest remains alive on the internet, with forums dedicated to the case where people discuss every known detail of the murders and come up with ever wilder suggestions about his identity. It's also inspired a variety of books, movies and even music.

Novels

In 1969 Arthur La Bern wrote Goodbye Piccadilly, Farewell Leicester Square, The plot centers on a serial killer in London who strangles his victims with his necktie. It's set just after the

war and the killer's friend, who is falsely ac-
cused of the murders, is a former RAF bomber
pilot. In a memorable scene he is arrested and,
drunk and confused, tells the police he murdered people in Dresden. When asked how
many he answers, "Thousands." The novel was
later used as the basis for Hitchcock's movie
Frenzy.

Bad Penny Blues by Cathi Unwin is also inspired by the Stripper's crimes. In this case
Unwin stuck with the facts for the crimes themselves and blended the case into a story about
the social scene in 1960s London. The plot
brings in organized crime, radical politics and a
collection of artists as well as the killer and the
colorful group of police hunting him.

Non-Fiction Books

Several authors have written about the case,
all of them taking different approaches and
some of them developing their own theories
about it. Some of these have already been
mentioned. Others are worth looking at as well.

None of them contain the magic clue that reveals the Stripper's identity but they can all contribute something to understanding what London was like at that time and the effect the killings had on society.

Murder Was My Business is the 1973 autobiography of John Du Rose, who took over the case after O'Hara's death. A chapter is devoted to the Stripper. It's well worth a read both for his thoughts on this case and for the rest of his career as a Murder Squad detective.

Brian McConnell published the first book to deal exclusively with the Stripper in 1974. In Found Naked and Dead McConnell comes to the same conclusions as Du Rose. Written closest to the time of the killings when memories were still fresh, it is an engaging read.

David Seabrook's Jack of Jumps is a more recent – and more sensational – look at the case. Seabrook claimed to have had access to the police files on the Stripper, which of course would have given him a lot of useful pointers. However the book itself is light on details of the investigation, and Seabrook's conclusion that Cushway was the Stripper is hardly credible. If you have any sympathy at all for the victims Seabrook's portrayals of them are likely to be offensive.

Neil Milkins's 2001 work Who Was Jack The Stripper? is interesting because it introduces Harold Jones as a possible suspect. Milkins has done a lot of research, even seeking out the surviving children of victims. Many of his conclusions are based on coincidences but that doesn't prevent this being a fascinating and informative look at the case.

Movies

Alfred Hitchcock is rightly famous for his suspense movies, many of which drew inspiration from real life events. For example Rope was based on the 1924 murder of Bobby Franks by Nathan Leopold and Richard Loeb. For his 1972 film Frenzy he started with the novel Goodbye Piccadilly, Farewell Leicester Square. The novel wasn't an exact retelling of the Stripper case but it was based on it, so the nude murders indirectly inspired Hitchcock's movie.

Music

The 1970 Black Sabbath album Paranoid contains a track titled Jack the Stripper/Fairies Wear Boots. The song itself doesn't have much connection with the case – it appears to have been written to tease skinheads after the band had a run-in with a group of them – but they did choose the killer's nickname for the title.

Of course the Stripper murders have left a legacy that goes beyond books, music and movies. They played a key role in changing police attitudes to prostitutes. The selling of sex is still deeply linked to crime in the UK, and the act itself is of borderline legality. The prostitutes themselves are looked on more as victims now, however. When they're murdered – and they still are, of course – it's taken a lot more seriously than it once would have been. By appealing for their help Commander Hatherill showed them that, when they were the victims of crime, the police would listen to them. The media, by highlighting the case, helped too. People began to see hookers as women, not just hookers. When Peter Sutcliffe started murdering prostitutes in 1975 the police response was rapid and massive. By 1977 Sutcliffe had expanded his targets to include any woman and, for the police and public alike, the distinction between prostitutes and "innocent" women practically disappeared. By making the deaths of streetwalkers a front page headline Jack the Stripper had played a large part in setting that process in motion. Attitudes still haven't changed completely but at least they're heading in the right direction.

www.ingramcontent.com/pod-product-compliance
Lightning Source LLC
Chambersburg PA
CBHW051037030426
42336CB00015B/2913